Designing

Entrances

for

Retail

and

Restaurant

Spaces

ROCKPORT

First published in the
United States of America by
Rockport Publishers, Inc.
33 Commercial Street
Gloucester, Massachusetts
01930-5089
Telephone: (978) 282-9590
Facsimile: (978) 283-2742

Distributed to the book trade and
art trade in the United States by
North Light Books, an imprint
of F & W Publications
1507 Dana Avenue
Cincinnati, Ohio 45207
Telephone: (800) 289-0963

Other Distribution by
Rockport Publishers, Inc.
Gloucester, Massachusetts
01930-5089

ISBN 1-56496-482-5
10 9 8 7 6 5 4 3 2 1

Book Design: Nassar Design
Art Director: Nélida Nassar
Designer: Margarita Encomienda

Cover Image:
Metropolitan Restaurant
Photo Credit:
Douglas Kahn

Printed in China.

To Sana – Our Radiance

Thanks are due to:

Jordan Mozer and Paula Jean Hoffman for the enthusiasm and

energy they put into the project;

Jeanine Caunt at Rockport Publishers for her patience and tact;

My sister Amla for her generous and expert advice;

my husband Tarik, as always, for his support;

and my two-year-old daughter Sana, without whose delicious diversions

this book would have been completed much, much earlier.

Designing Entrances for Retail and Restaurant Spaces

GLOUCESTER MASSACHUSETTS

ROCKPORT PUBLISHERS

Nayana Currimbhoy

CONTENTS

Nayana Currimbhoy **INTRODUCTION**

Our relatives lived in a traditional mansion, or *haveli,* in the old part of town. In Western India, the haveli is a traditional home consisting of clusters of two-story structures built around a large open courtyard. Ours had an immense entrance; an elephant with a ceremonial seat atop its back could walk through it at weddings. The weathered wooden gate was opened only for weddings, deaths, and prayer ceremonies. For everyday use, there was a tiny little doorway–it would let in one person at a time–carved at the lower left-hand corner of the gate. The little door, which had a threshold to keep out wandering cows and dogs, was usually ajar during the day. When we went to visit, we would poke our heads in, and my grandmother would ask the children playing in the dust if our relatives were home.

I don't remember who we met, what we ate, or what we spoke about on those visits. But yet, we loved to go with my grandmother to the haveli. The excitement of those visits started with the entryway. First, there was the vast difference in scale between the ceremonial entrance and the tiny everyday entrance; the expanse of the large door suggested that our passage through it would magically transform us into bigger, taller beings. Then, there was the experience of entry. It was a passage into another world. The old town was a crush of shops and cows and carts and cars; and then, suddenly, stepping over the threshold, you would see the old women shelling peas on the stoop, or a young girl squirming as her mother tied her hair into tight braids.

Photos, this page:
Tarik Currimbhoy

Photo:
Tarik Currimbhoy

Public entrances, private entrances, exclusive entrances, ceremonial entrances. In places of worship the threshold takes on a metaphorical significance. Having crossed it, you are in the presence of God. You prepare yourself to meet the deity before you pass through the door. In Hindu temples you remove your shoes at the threshold; in mosques, churches, and synagogues you cover your hair. The Taj Mahal is made up of a progression of entrances. The first is an arched entrance which frames the building. Then, as one walks past the canal to the tomb, one passes through a grand, carved entrance. The importance of the building is revealed through the ceremony of the entrances. The palaces of the east were built like Chinese boxes, with a progression of gateways that led from the pomp and splendor of the public spaces to the luxury and eccentricities of private boudoirs and baths. There were no signs or labels. The shape, size and structure of the doorway told the story.

Photo:
© Vincent Fressola

Photo:
© Vincent Fressola

The entrances in this book tell stories. They sell dreams of power, grace and pleasure; they offer mysteries. Although they face each other in this book in pristine competition, they often exist cheek by jowl with chaotic urban realities. Built near bomb sites, upon ancient ruins, surrounded by the pungent smell of drying fish, or adjacent to fluorescent massage parlors, this somewhat random collection of malls, stores, and restaurants from disparate towns and cities speak a common language. The entrances employ an international vocabulary of universally recognizable symbols to create a message. Arm yourself with hope, they say, all ye who enter here.

Photos, this page:
Tarik Currimbhoy

Jordan Mozer **FOREWORD**

Through the window, gusts of almost-autumn evening air and the peeling of taxi tires on the pavement to O'Hare, the patter of familiar billboards and retail constructions...I'm up, anxious to compare overseas client with what we have deciphered from fax notes and accented calls, excited to build my own stories in a foreign country.

My enthusiasm is numbed by hours of dull engine roar and gray recycled air, cramped by a cold search for sleep in the painful airplane seat...Finally it comes, velvet and anesthetic, heavy with dreams of discovery.

I am startled awake by an illegible public address, the bumping onto tarmac, and a hard march through a smoky terminal.

Propped up on luggage and bitter airport espresso in my client's Jeep Cherokee, we drive by rotting medieval walls that contain the city center. I struggle with a fuzzy sense of time, the brightness of the sun and volume and asymmetry of American rock-and-roll on the radio. We discuss the project, and I try to express coherent ideas about the evolution free-style American casual dining, but the blurry city reeling whispers distractions...

This is not my shiny new hundred-year-old hometown of crystal objects in a grid. Here are ancient curved avenues sized for horse carts instead of cars, hand sculpted stone facades saturated with histories and squeezed up against one another to make rhythmic roofless rooms of streets which open onto landmarks and vistas.

Glancing down to the base of these worn streetrooms is an MTV jump cut from a historical documentary to a Fellini parade of elegantly tailored motorcars and crowds against flirting shop fronts punctuated with seductive signs. The ground floor is alive with popular modernisms infused with Regional Once Upon a Time. This surreal juxtaposition amplifies the possibility of adventure, counterpoint to chain-stuffed suburban malls at home...

Some are coy, aloof and restrained, overture to expensively handmade pleasures inside...Others are forward, reckless and titillating, promising an ephemeral burning celebrity, unexpected romance. One is artfully cluttered with dusty mysteries, antiquities. A precocious cafe facade conjures the myth salons peopled by irreverent youth, articulate and wildly talented. These facades at once suggest permanence and the ferocious perpetual change, containers of seasonally mutating menus and collections; it could all vaporize in the mist of early morning.

After meetings, I shower and scrape the beard off my face. The insidious streetscape inspires an illusion of need, a compulsion to explore the restaurants and shops despite my exhaustion, inflaming a submerged instinct to hunt for rare products, ephemeral moments, an urgent modern wish to record this journey with consumption.

The Street swallows me; a daggerboard of bread aromas foreshadow a muscular wooden bakery door; the eyes of iced fish and terraco diners peek out from vine wrapped wrought iron; a jewler works goldwire next to gemstones in a cast bronze framed window, techno music and a dreamy vignette behind seamless plate glass invite entrance to a glossy Vogue magazine world.

The intoxication is complete; my eyes surf the facades for original objects, analyzing mutations and figature of semi-familiar forms. I track the fair or famous. I fear that I am missing something.

An intimate doorway beguiles me with idiosyncratic details that anticipate a story inside. The hand-built door is heavy—the pull caresses my hand. The vestibule immerses me in a muffled darkness paneled with the same hand-built door details; compressing down to a small door. I tug at it, surprised to stop onto a balcony overlooking a sumptuous soaring variation on the entry space richly lighted, a space that poses new questions.

Photo:

Paul Warchol

It is said that in remote corners of the world, you can use a pair of Levi's jeans as currency. Levi's, Nike, Coca-Cola—these are the globally sought-after products, the products that confer confidence and status on an individual by their very use. Now, at the end of the millennium, these have become household words around the world, the common language that transcends barriers of race and region.

THE COMMERCIAL LANDSCAPE

The superstore is a relative newcomer to the commercial landscape. In the early 1990s corporations like Nike decided that they needed more than brand recognition: they wanted a corporate presence. Thus was born the superstore. The superstore, as the name suggests, aims to be bigger and better than other stores. As in the Levi's and Nike stores shown in this chapter, the superstore is usually a stand-alone store located in a prestigious metropolitan area. The streetfront of the superstore establishes its corporate identity. Therefore the entrances are usually grand, speaking of power and money. The superstore sells more than just shoes, T-shirts, and jeans—it sells a corporate identity.

Chain stores and restaurants have been a ubiquitous feature in the American landscape ever since McDonald's first raised its yellow arches. Less obvious, perhaps, are the chains that began to thrive in the nineties: small boutiques that sell high-end luxury items by a single designer or manufacturer, located in several countries. Exemplified by Bottega Veneta and Kate Spade, as featured in this chapter, these chains create a distinctive image as much by their design as by the products they sell.

Photo:
Steve Hall/Hedrich Blessing

BOTTEGA VENETA

Project
Bottega Veneta stores

Architect
François de Menil

Photographer
Paul Warchol

These shops were designed by François de Menil for Bottega Veneta, an Italian luxury leather-goods company. The project's goals were to make the shop an organic part of the acquisition experience and to use the architecture as the display. The boutiques, whether freestanding or located in department stores, feature clean, contemporary design and are memorable for their creative maximization of space and rigorous attention to detail.

The challenge was to use the architecture to redefine the role of the interior as the display. The mediating zone of traditional window displays was removed to make the interior fully visible from outside. The interior architecture and the merchandise displays together forge a strong visual identity for the store that makes traditional window dressing unnecessary. In addition, the removal of visual boundaries creates the illusion of an expansive interior. Planar cabinetry elements and lighting manipulate the relationship among floor, walls, and ceiling; they break preconceived spatial boundaries by alluding to space beyond the visible edges. The cabinetry floats above the floor, disappears into the ceiling, and frames views. Floating or freestanding, these layered elements expand the viewer's perception of the store's limits.

The materials palette of medium-density fiberboard (MDF), ebonized wood, glass, stone, and concrete, and the construction detailing contribute to the overall aesthetic of elegance and simplicity.

The four shops featured here are located in New York; Short Hills, New Jersey; Boston; and Fukuoka, Japan. While they share both a palette and a philosophical approach, each is a unique variation on the theme as dictated by site specifics.

In Short Hills, New Jersey,
a triangular site resulted in a
curved-glass enclosing wall
that maximizes frontage.

At the Copley Place Mall,
Boston, a long, narrow site is
given visual elbow room by the
custom corrugated-glass entrance
at one side and a display box
inserted into the glass facade.

In Solaria Plaza, Fukuoka,
Japan, the trademark display
wall becomes the storefront
itself.

Solaria Plaza is a freestanding
storefront at a prestigious
corner location.

NIKETOWN

Projects
Niketown

Locations
New York, NY USA
Seattle, WA USA

Designer
Nike Design Team

Photographer
Steve Hall/
Hedrich Blessing

Nike's answer to the superstores of the 1990s is Niketown, a multistory, freestanding building selling Nike products and accessories and providing sports-related services to the local community.

The most impressive of the Niketowns is the flagship store off Madison Avenue in midtown Manhattan, opened in November 1996. The impressive entrance is reminiscent of early twentieth-century gymnasiums. Here, at Niketown, the entryway is deceptive: although it establishes a sports vocabulary, it gives no hint of the futuristic store nestled within.

As conceived by a Nike team led by Gordon Thompson, vice president of design, and John Hoke, image design creative director, the store is a building within a building—a ship in a bottle. The exterior building (the bottle) is reminiscent of a classic New York school gymnasium, its entrance emphasized by a grand arch. Inside is a completely freestanding modern structure (the ship) that houses five retail floors—66,520 square feet (5,987 square meters) of retail selling space.

The two buildings come together in an atrium; at this juncture, the store goes through a metamorphosis, transforming the sensory experience elicited. Every fifteen minutes a bit of drama occurs when a screen descends over the front arched window and atrium skylight, dimming interior light levels. Skybox windows open, and a three-minute Nike film is projected onto a three-story media screen. A Nike clock, inspired by sports scoreboards, counts down to the next showing.

Along with Nike sports products,
Niketown New York features
sports archives and memorabilia,
as well as a huge flipper board
which gives up-to-the-minute
sports scores from around
the world.

Aiming to be a meeting place
and information center for local
athletes, Niketown New York
offers interactive displays on
great athletes, an athletic Bio
Tower CD ROM display, as well
as a staffed desk providing information about local sports events.

Niketown New York is one of
seven Niketowns in the United
States, the company is planning
to expand into cities in Europe
and Canada.

Niketown, Seattle, a 24,000-square foot (2,160-square-meter) store, was a part of the rebirth of the city's downtown area. It features archival audio and video presentations and large posters of Northwestern athletes.

GALLERY

The external steel framing of the
entrance to the Virgin Megastore
in Orlando, designed by the Los
Angeles architectural firm SPF:a,
evokes the excitement of a rock-
concert stage.

Photos, this page:
Mark Lohman

The canopy, which is ingeniously
constructed on stage lifts, offers a
venue for live performances. The
metal framework is scaled up to
support large signs that are visible from a distance.

A corner site at the ground level on Lexington Avenue in Manhattan, the flagship Original Levi's store by Bergmeyer Associates features large graphic images alternating with the universally recognized Levi's logo. A light box above every window creates a nighttime street presence.

Photos, this page:
Chun Y. Lai

A red wall flanking the entrance goes all the way up to the third floor, uniting the three-level facade of the Original Levi's store in midtown Manhattan.

At the Gant store on Fifth
Avenue in Manhattan, designed
by Bergmeyer Associates, a 38-
foot-high (11.6-meter-high) clear-
glass storefront creates a show-
case for the company's clothing
collection. Lighting, program-
med to change according to the
time of day and year, creates a
unified billboard effect.

Photo:
Chun Y. Lai

In the Vista Ridge Shopping Center in Lewisville, Texas, two tapered concrete columns covered with a mosaic-like composition of broken tiles support a curved canopy that defines the entrance to Larry's Shoes.

Photos, this page:
Scott Kohno

Designed by the California firm of C & J Partners, the facade of Larry's Shoes pairs earth tones with colorful, modern-art graphics to create a zany, upbeat look at relatively low cost.

Kate Spade is a chain of boutiques that sells designer handbags. The success of the first store in Soho in New York City led to the opening of ten additional shops in Japan and one in Los Angeles.

Photos, this page:
Lynne Massimo

In this witty entrance by New York Architects Rogers Marvel, a perpendicular wall extension jutting outward represents a pocketbook handle.

The extrusion, used by Rogers
Marvel again in the larger Fire
Street shop in Tokyo, became a
signature element for the sophisticated Kate Spade chain.

Photos:
Itochu Fashion System

The recently opened store in
Los Angeles. In all the Kate
Spade stores, the entry "handle"
has a center panel containing a
window art exhibit that is never
a handbag.

Photo:
Dominique Vorillon

Agnona, located on Madison Avenue–one of the prime retail streets in the world–is the first U.S. venture of an exclusive Italian cashmere clothing designer, manufacturer, and retail organization.

Photos, this page:
Peter Paige

Designed by Gleicher Design Group, along with Studio Gardino Architectural from Italy, and Larry S. Davis and Associates, the store is a clean, modern space in which luxurious material such as pearwood floors, sanded glass cabinetry, and Carrara marble wall panels act as a counterpoint to the "soft" luxury of the cashmere products being sold. In the tradition of exclusive Madison Avenue boutiques, the entrance of the narrow, 750 square foot shop acts as a life-size "picture-frame" surrounded by a wide band of polished steel.

The strong herringbone pattern of the wide plank rift cut white oak floor visually draws the customer into the store. The entry floor consists of a warm cream-colored limestone display area with a custom inlay stainless steel grill.

Photo:

Sandro Raffone

In Naples, Italy, Chiffon an upscale fashion boutique by architect and Professor Sandro Raffone has an entrance that extends itself onto the sidewalk, offering bypassers oblique views into the space.

Photos, this page:
Sandro Raffone

The curved lines that dominate the exterior are continued in the interior with a spectacular curved staircase in which the steel bars of the exterior are used as a handrail.

The two-story store makes a vertical statement on the street with a balcony window at the second level. Curved steel bars separate the shop from the busy street front.

The Gansevoort Gallery entrance works on an ingenuous pivoting lever arm counterbalanced by an 800 pound weight which draws the gate upward. The storefront, designed by Ali Tayar of Parallel Design Partnership draws its vocabulary from the loading docks and dented metal awnings of Manhattan's meat packing district.

Photos, this page:
Joshua McHugh

The gate is fabricated from punched aluminum sections adapted from industrial catwalks. When open, it reveals a large glass panel that takes up most of the furniture store's width. The panel pivots open to serve as a loading dock.

Restaurants and retail have two elements in common: they are to be used for a specific purpose and for a short time. It is specifically because of this—the limited range of activities engaged in for a limited amount of time—that the designer of such structures can be fanciful in creating the environment.

It is possible to bring the heightened reality of theater to the everyday experiences of eating and shopping.

DESIGN AS THEATER

Employing drama and fantasy, the projects in this chapter feature environments that entertain and excite.

Drawing their inspiration from literature, myth, and music, designers play with form and scale, in creating the facade, entryway, and interior using saturated colors and unusual shapes to create the unexpected. In Amnesia, the designers, building on the well-loved *Alice in Wonderland* theme, flank an overscaled door with a mysterious circular box-office cashier. In Iridium, intricate custom-metal forms attempt to express music visually. From the moment one steps in the door, transformation has occurred. The visitor is transported to an altered state of being, physically and emotionally.

Photo:
Alessandro Ciampi

Designer of the famous Planet Hollywood clubs, David Rockwell, whose Official All Star Café in this chapter is driven by the star-power of famous sportsmen, talks about the role of theater in architecture:

"Much of our work has centered on entertainment architecture, and on the notion of architecture as theater. The theatrical aspect of individuals proceeding through space is examined and emphasized by focusing on the vital roles lighting, decoration, and special effects play in creating every set. We concentrate on designing environments that give the visitor a feeling of being transported to another place in time."

CLUB CABOOL

Project
Club Cabool

Location
St. Louis, MO USA

Architect
Ray M. Simon

Consultants
Lorens Holm (design)
Robin Nelson (materials)

Owner/Designer
Paul Guzzardo

Photographer
Steve Hall/
Hedrich Blessing

The unusual double entrance to Club Cabool in St. Louis, Missouri, is a result of history filtered through the perception of an architect. The 1521 Building, which was a factory at the turn of the century, was to be turned into club and bar. But removal of the flat-tile storefront uncovered remains of a classical revivalist facade, its twin arches outlined by the patched scars of once-projecting terra-cotta ornamentation. "This discovery suggested a design approach that preserves the original architectural elements in their transformed state while inserting the new construction in such a way so as to explore the relationship between authentic and simulated, perceived and represented," says architect Ray Simon.

The battered facade's ruinlike quality was retained and highlighted with illumination. A new glass-block and steel storefront was constructed, recessed and oblique to the original facade, creating a space between the original facade and the new entrance. The result is a mysterious, layered entryway made up of light and shadow, old and new, past and present.

The architect retained the industrial nature of the interior. Concrete floors and columns, exposed mechanical ducts and chutes were painted, polished, and highlighted. The original sloping concrete floor was used as a design element and referred to again in the sloping bar and slanted steel wall.

The unexpected mix of styles and periods in the entrance to Club Cabool piques the interest. It is impossible to tell what the interior will be like...

As in the exterior, the design of the interior has been guided by the nature of the space. The industrial nature of the space has been highlighted. The floor, which was sloped (probably to facilitate deliveries) has been highlighted. Artist Robin Nelson has built a sloping wall which is designed to work has a sculpture in the space.

Deep, saturated colors add a striking contrast to the raw finishes and fixtures of the otherwise stark space.

RISTORANTE L'ARCA

Project
Ristorante L'Arca

Location
Follonica, Italy

Designer
Antonello Boschi,
Architect

Photographer
Alessandro Ciampi

For architect Antonello Boschi wharves and piers are the most romantic way of interacting with the sea. "They are better than ships," he says, "because you do not have to abandon your ties with the land; they are better than the beach, because the relation with the sea is total and complete." The bar and nightclub L' Arca *(the ark)* is a wooden building perched precariously above the sea in the small town of Follonica, Italy, designed to awaken the romance of leaning out toward the open sea and defying the winds.

From the wharf a steel sculpture, a kind of fin, with *L' Arca* embedded in it, draws attention to the restaurant and nightclub. A teakwood bench runs parallel to the gangway. The design of L'Arca was inspired by the ship *Andrea Doria*, designed by Gio Ponti in 1952, and by Pulitzer Finelli's designs for the great liners built between the world wars. Streamlined shapes in polished steel—the fin of the exterior is repeated again in the bar area, the outdoor lamps, the signs, and the furniture—refer to the interior of a ship, while a meticulous attention to detail raises the project to the level of art.

This nightclub takes cues from the romance of travel on the open sea. A steel "fin" anchored to the wharf serves as a facade–or interface–to draw passersby.

The space is used as a restaurant, bar and concert hall. The differences in activity are implied through subtle changes in lighting and materials.

The quality and intensity of light is altered to meet the needs of the space: soft wall sconces in the bar, halogen and hanging lamps in the concert area, and a prominent, decorative, custom light fixture in the dining area.

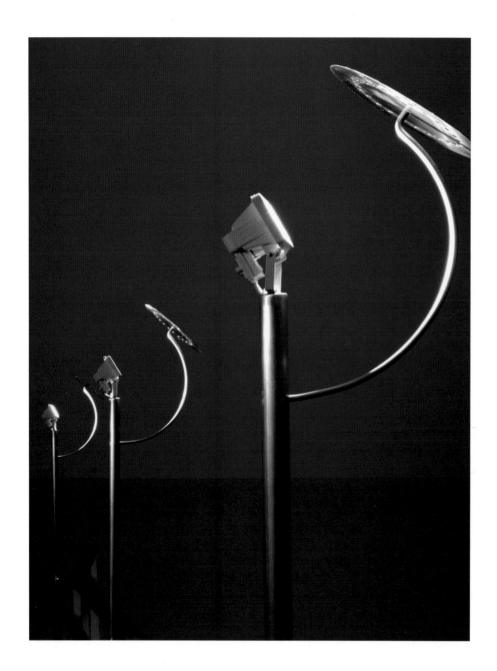

GALLERY

For Props in Charlotte, North Carolina, the Shook Design Group renovated an abandoned restaurant and added a highly visible exterior awning system with reversed silhouette letters to announce the new interior.

Photos, this page:
Tim Buchman

A larger-than-lifesize jack-in-the-box hangs from the ceiling at Props and greets visitors as they walk through the door. A series of living-room vignettes around the room encourage social interaction.

On Sunset Strip in Los Angeles, the facade of Billboard Live features a video marquee that displays a changing array of moving images. Frosted-glass panels behind the videos change color in this traffic-stopping design by Jeremy Railton and Thomas Mahler of the Last Design Company.

Photo:
Tom Bonner

Rockwell Group's Official All Star Café in the heart of New York City's Times Square is a splashy, stadiumlike restaurant with sports memorabilia, state-of-the-art interactive television, and virtual-reality video. The entrance, with its larger-than-life billboard, makes the Café's presence known in the jostled atmosphere of Times Square.

Photo:
Norman McGrath

Aiming to make the visitor
forget the stresses of daily life,
Amnesia, a club and cafe in
Toronto designed by II BY IV
Design Associates, plays with
scale and form. A circular cashier
flanked by a pair of vibrantly
upholstered doors dominates
the foyer.

Photo:
David Whittaker

Conceived and realized by Walt Disney Imagineering, the first DisneyQuest™ facility opened in Orlando, Florida in June 1998. The 10,000 square foot (929 square meter), five-story building designed by Walt Disney Imagineering in conjunction Jordan Mozer and Associates, has a bright blue wave facade, emblazoned with a prominent "hurricane Mickey," a swirling variation of the classic mouse icon.

Credit:
© Disney Enterprises, Inc.

Via a narrow vestibule and an elevator ride, visitors come upon an imposing five-story atrium from which radiate the entrances to four zones of entertainment. Conceived as an entrance to the crossroads of adventure, the atrium, dominated by navigational instruments from the age of discovery, is designed to create a magical environment.

Credit:
© Disney Enterprises, Inc.

The Wonderland Café draws upon the *Alice in Wonderland* theme to create a fantastic setting in which shapes and sizes are distorted. The carpet, with its dense, hieroglyphic pattern has no repeat. It was designed specifically for the project by Jordan Mozer and Associates, and was manufactured by Miliken.

Credit:
© Disney Enterprises, Inc.

The act of arrival is a theatrical experience at Taboo. The street-front window contains elaborate antique wrought iron gates salvaged from a movie set, so that passersby get a tantalizing glimpse of the inside. Oversized red-stained doors whose gothic arches frame wired glass inserts backed with steel grilles lead into the entrance area.

Photo:
David Whittaker

In Taboo, a nightclub in the basement of a Toronto office building, II BY IV Design Associates created a warm, flamboyant, and romantic atmosphere with strong Victorian overtones.

Walls, flooring ceiling, uphol-
stery and woodwork of the entry
foyer to this 10,000 square-foot
(929 square-meter) nightclub are
in lush red tones.

Photos, this page:
David Whittaker

Across from Lincoln Center in Manhattan, the cultural mecca for opera, symphony, ballet, and dramatic-theater devotees, is Iridium, a restaurant and jazz club inspired by the performing arts and, according to its designer, Jordan Mozer, "infused with the logic of a dream or a poem."

Photos, this page:
David Clifton

In Iridium's entryway an arched copper canopy, a leaping menu box, and a stretching window perform a graceful dance.

Throughout the space, sculptural and graphic representations of music abound.

Once inside, bowing arches continue the performance while cast-aluminum balusters represent the musical idea of counterpoint.

Photos, this page:
David Clifton

A successful Los Angeles nightclub and restaurant, The Garden
of Eden, designed by Margaret
O'Brien of O'Brien Associates,
draws its inspiration from
Morocco.

Photos, this page:
David Glomb

The designer and the client,
David Judaken, a young South
African ex-patriot for whom the
nightclub is the realization of
an ambitious dream, traveled
to Morocco with the designer
to source the lamps, fabrics, and
artifacts used in the dramatic
entryway, and in the interior.

The idea, according to the
designer, was not to build a
"Moroccan" nightclub, but to
infuse the nightclub with the
heady, exotic feeling of being
in a cultured, ancient city.

The building itself was essentially
a concrete bunker with two
concrete supports in the middle
of the space. Beginning with
the entryway, the designers created different levels to generate
excitement.

The Landmark Hotel in London is a 1897 hotel recently remodeled by Hirsch Bedner Associates of Santa Monica, California. In the six story Wintergarden, full sized palm trees function as a theatrical entrance.

Photos, this page:
Robert Miller

Larger than life antique garden ironwork ornaments act as a congenial waiting area overlooking the Wintergarden.

Photo:
Grant Mudford

Bold impact is the magic formula for the design of fast-food places. Clamoring for attention on the suburban strip, such restaurants have but an instant to attract attention. And the first clue as to what an establishment is like on the interior is what is being established on the exterior. The entrance is all-important; it serves up in- stant recognition. The order is for speed and convenience, not for adventure and romance.

HIGH SPEED

Accordingly, the design of fast-food establishments is traditionally built on the familiar. The trick is to create variations within the genre. As seen at the Cotton Street Diner, variations on the humble American diner employ period themes to create nostalgia. Another successful technique is the narrative theme. In both the Rainforest Cafe and the Flying Fish Café, shown in this chapter, an oversized, topical entrance installation not only adds zest and color but shouts for attention.

In *Learning from Las Vegas* Robert Venturi noted the successful formula for "commercial vernacular": an oversized sign that can be seen at high speed, a low one-story structure set back off the highway, and a large parking lot in front. Twenty years have passed since Venturi wrote this seminal text. Restaurant design has changed and evolved, but the fast-food restaurants along the American suburban strip remain frozen in time, as if ordained by some divine law. A rare—and welcome—variation is the Kentucky Fried Chicken (KFC) in Los Angeles. A structure that not only breaks the overt rules—it is a two-story structure set next to the highway with parking at the back—the building also makes a statement about our fast-food culture. The owner of the franchise and the architect of the building had the courage to create good design along the suburban strip. We can only hope that more franchises will follow suit. Wouldn't it be nice to drive along the highway and actually see interesting facades?

Photo:
Roderick Coyne

LA FRÉGATE

Project
La Frégate

Location
St. Helier, Jersey, England

Designers
Alsop & Störmer
Architects with
Mason Design

Photographer
Roderick Coyne

Client
Jersey Waterfront
Enterprise Board

The seaside town of St. Helier in Jersey, one of the Channel Islands off the coast of England, has been a tourist attraction since Victorian times. A seaside cafe had existed there before World War II. The new cafe, La Frégate, completed in August 1997, is a part of a larger development project for Jersey's Waterfront Enterprise Board that will include a hotel, housing, and a leisure complex.

Designed by the British architecture firm of Alsop & Störmer with Mason Design, this beautiful seaside cafe is curved both in plan and section. Its glass roof projects at the sides and cantilevers at both ends of the building. Conceived originally by William Alsop as a seafood cafe with a fishlike form, the building developed into a timber structure resembling an inverted boat. With its curved underbelly raised on recessed columns within a hard landscaped oval ditch, the hull of La Frégate appears to float.

The entryways to the restaurant are as inspired as its shape. Access from the external deck and gardens into the cafe is through two large gull-wing doors that fold open like drawbridges or by two short steel-and-timber bridges.

La Frégate, which has a prominent waterfront location, seats
72 people inside, and 120 in the
outdoor section.

The interior area is splashed with natural light from the skylight which runs along the spine of the building.

Boat builders and craftsmen were
employed as consultants while
creating the curved steel structure
clad in weatherproofed timber.

KENTUCKY FRIED CHICKEN

Project
Kentucky Fried Chicken

Location
Los Angeles, CA USA

Designer
Jeffrey Daniels
(Formerly Grinstein/
Daniels Architects)

Photographer
Grant Mudford

The Kentucky Fried Chicken on Western Avenue in Los Angeles plays with form and scale to create a witty building that is at once an advertisement for a popular chain and a commentary on our fast-food culture.

The client, a franchisee of Kentucky Fried Chicken and a collector of contemporary art, retained Grinstein/ Daniels Architects to create a building that would make a statement. Although the restaurant is unlike the regular KFC franchises that dot the country, the client got approval for the unusual structure by taking a model to KFC's Louisville headquarters.

The narrow site, which had to accommodate parking as well as a drive-through, suggested a two-story structure. The architect decided to depart from the norm by placing the building in front and the parking at the back. The curving facade (which resembles a KFC bucket) emerged as a way to facilitate the movement of cars around the building. The giant window creates a theatrical facade and a light-filled interior. The storefront entrance, which wraps around the building, creates transparency.

"The building presents itself without apology as an urban sign along a commercial strip. It attempts to strike a difficult balance between the all-too-familiar logos of its populist product and the lingering memory of constructivism's early experiments in creating a new populist iconography," says architect Jeffrey Daniels.

This unusual fast food restaurant is the result of one man's perseverance. The client, who was already a successful and well-respected KFC franchisee, believed in the venture enough to physically take the model to the KFC headquarters and convince the corporate team.

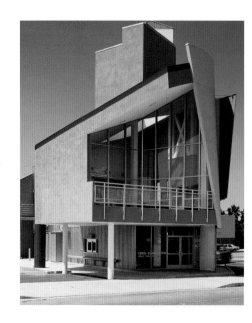

To accomadate both parking and drive-in on the narrow site, the architect placed the building in front and parking at the back.

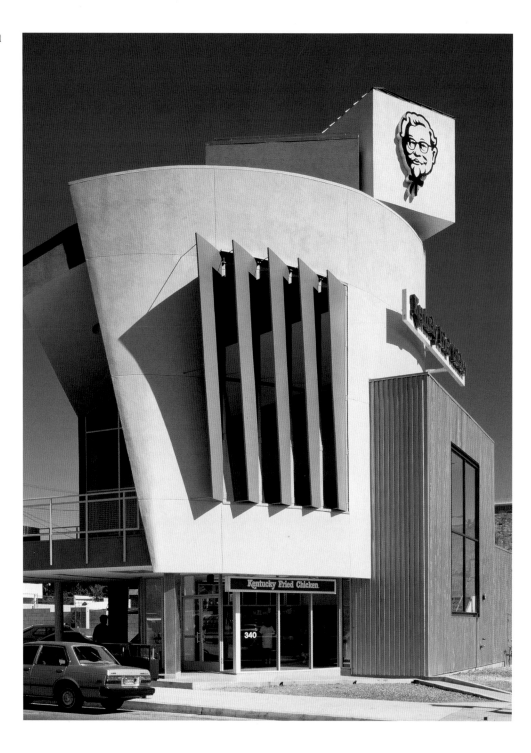

The architect has very deliberately attempted to expand the boundaries of the fast food genre. The design has been successful.

GALLERY

A quirky two-story red steel tower marks the corner entrance of the Anodyne@43rd Coffee-house in Minneapolis like "a commercial counterpart to an ecclesiastical bell tower," according to designer Geoffrey Warner of Alchemy Design. Like bells, steel coffee cups strung on aircraft cable sway in the breeze.

Photos, this page:
Karen Melvin

The tower, a wry comment on the enormous billboards and large neon signs of the surrounding industrial neighborhood, supports the coffeehouse signage, made of digitally printed white fabric stretched taut like a sail.

A 20-foot-long (6.2-meter-long) airplane wing acts as Anodyne's canopy, tying the coffeehouse with its location along the airport route. The interior contains industrial finishes and found objects such as a canoe paddle, oxidized copper, rubber, steel floor plates, and printing-press letters.

Photo:

Karen Melvin

The literal interpretation of the theme in the Rainforest Cafe in Westbury, Connecticut, by Daroff Design, lends more than a touch of humor to this 50-foot-high (15.2-meter-high) storefront.

Photo:
Elliott Kaufman

In Chicago, the Big Downtown by Lieber Cooper Associates recreates the ambiance of the swing era of the city's historic downtown area. The deco façade with its bright neon and bold graphics is built like a theater marquee.

Photo:
Mark Ballogg of
Steincamp/Ballogg

For the Cotton Street Diner
and coffee shop in Charlotte,
North Carolina, the Shook
Design Group changed the
exterior image by relocating
the main entry and introducing
a wide expanse of windows.

Photos, this page:
Tim Buchman

Taking advantage of the height
of the new structure, the designers inserted vertical wedges that
carry into the interior. Use of
details such as wooden venetian
blinds and signage successfully
create an exuberant period look.

The design objective was to create a period diner image. Low partitions, planters, and bright colors create an ambiance that offers a casual but intimate dining experience.

Photos, this page:
Tim Buchman

The 1930s period look is further enhanced by the use of large period movie posters, black and white photos of local and national figures from the time, and dated hubcaps for serving trays.

The Cheesecake Factory, a 17,000-square-foot (1,530 square-meter) restaurant specializing in cheese-cakes, is located in Chicago's John Hancock Building. Designer Jordan Mozer's baro-que copper addition to the facade created quite a stir, as it was perceived by some as defacing the city landmark.

Photos, this page:
David Clifton

Drawn from the shape of cheese-cake filling as it pours from tubes in the client's factory, the car-toonish copper forms outline the extended basement canopy of the Cheesecake Factory.

Detail of the ground-floor entrance and menu box, also constructed of copper.

The major part of the large cheesecake restaurant is located in the basement. The theatrical and controversial facades of the entries at the ground floor and basement serve to draw attention to the relatively small frontage of the restaurant.

Photos, this page:
David Clifton

The voluptuous forms and exciting finishes of the interior of the Cheesecake Factory live up to its tantalizing entrance.

Photo:
David Clifton

Old garages, abandoned warehouses, derelict bodegas— in this chapter are examples of all of these, turned into successful restaurants and stores. When the function changes, so must the face. The most common way is with canopies, signs, and banners. But good design is good business, and an altered, revitalized facade is a sure way to signal a change within.

When intervening on the street front, three options **FACE LIFTS** are open to the designer: restore and adapt, but retain the identity of the original; highlight some features of the old, but introduce new elements to create a definite new personality; or create a space with its own internal logic that relates only marginally to the rhythm of the surrounding reality.

A sampling of restaurants and stores from cities as disparate as Zagreb, Naples, New York City, and Salt Lake City provide examples of successful facelifts. In older and denser cities, where the original facade had a street identity and a relationship to its neighbors, as did the Ban Cafe, on a Zagreb city square whose history dates back to the seventeenth century, and as did Paci, built in a landmark railway station in Connecticut, the challenge to the designer is to restore the facade and maintain the integrity of the original space while creating an entrance that piques the interest and marks a new function within.

Photo:
Douglas Kahn

METROPOLITAN RESTAURANT

Project
Metropolitan Restaurant

Location
Salt Lake City, UT USA

Designer
Louis Ulrich
FFKR Architects/Planners

Photographer
Douglas Kahn

Owner
The Olson Family

The designer, owner, and chef of this sophisticated Salt Lake City restaurant were clear about one thing: They wanted a restaurant that represented their city. "We did not want a fashion statement about other cities," says Louis Ulrich of FFKR Architects/Planners. They achieved this through the use of bold, unusual forms, juxtaposed with a straightforward use of materials.

The restaurant is located in a 1950s garage building located in the city's downtown warehouse district. The original front had been a garage door and a cinder block facade. The architects removed the original facade–the existing bowstring trusses remain–and inserted instead, an open glass and aluminum facade that invites people to look in.

In addition, a curved concrete wall juts out onto the street and flags bypassers. Moving into the building, the wall becomes a screened panel specially created for the space by local artisan Michael Hullet. The screen serves to separate the bar and lounge area from the restaurant. In the kitchen area, the wall changes again into concrete, signaling another function. "It's a kind of visual slice into the building," says Ulrich.

Additional details such as the use of glass cylinders in the curved concrete wall, and sandblasted industrial sash windows all add up to create a special restaurant which was a James Beard Award Finalist.

Designer Louis Ulrich removed
the garage door and built an elegant glass front that opened up
the restaurant. A curved concrete
wall extends beyond the glass
facade, creating an additional
area of interest.

Designed by FKKR Architects/
Planners, the Metropolitan
Restaurant in downtown Salt
Lake City was created from a
structure originally built in the
1950s as an auto mechanic's
garage.

The existing structure of the Metropolitan Cafe was removed and replaced with an aluminum and glass facade. "During the construction, people thought we were crazy. They kept saying 'why don't they just tear the entire building down?'" says architect Louis Ulrich of FFKR.

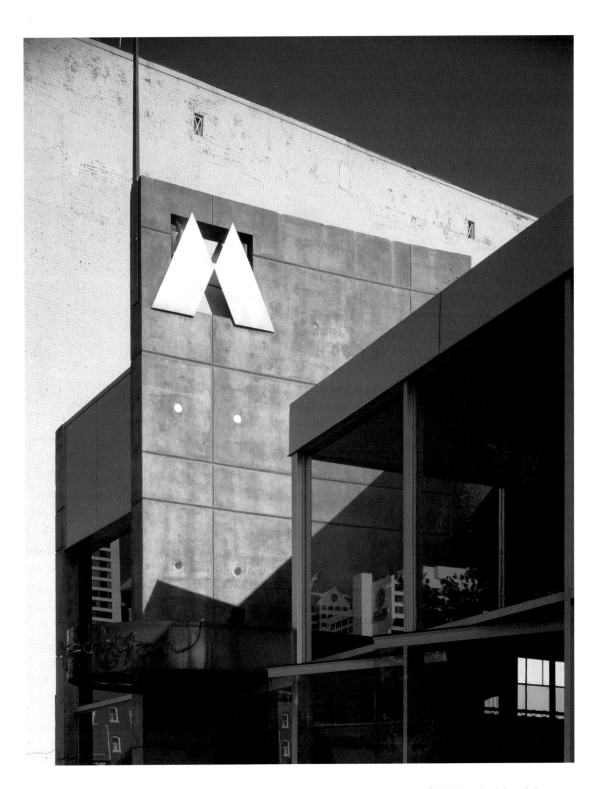

Ulrich retained the existing building because he wanted to retain the patina of the old building, a 1950s garage in downtown Salt Lake City, and juxtapose it with the new facade.

HUDSON CLUB

Project
Hudson Club

Location
Chicago, IL USA

Designer
Jordan Mozer &
Associates

Photographer
David Clifton

Take a 1940s supper club, add the inside of a luxury airplane, sprinkle in some references to streamline design for good measure, and shake vigorously. The result? The Hudson Club, one of the more successful night spots in Chicago.

Designed with flair, confidence, and a deft touch by Chicago designer Jordan Mozer, the Hudson Club manages to combine the plush and seductive ambience of a supper club with the excitement of flight and speed.

The facade of the single-story, airplane hangar–type warehouse was substantially altered. A sleek aluminum-and-glass storefront with a 28-foot-long by 8-foot-high (8.5-meter-long by 2.4-meter-high) elliptical storefront window frames the activity inside. Two large light-reflecting aluminum wings project into the street.

In the interior, clever references to flight—skewed circular windows that graphically portray high speed, aluminum and blown-glass taillights, abstracted forms of wings, fenders, and propellers—permeate the design. Aluminum hardware and seating frames suggest airships; plush fabrics and saturated colors add a touch of old-world elegance to this sleek and successful space.

The long, low building with its bowstring trusses suggests an airplane hangar. The designers have capitalized on this to create a restaurant inspired by ideas of flight from 1930s industrial design.

Continuing the airplane hangar
theme, the interior of the
Hudson Club is a long room
with an emphasis on horizontal
elements.

Furniture and fixtures are bent
and skewed suggesting the dis-
tortion caused by high speed.
The mirror above the bar is egg
shaped, the bar stools and metal
railings are "lunging" and the
entrance door has a skewed
porthole.

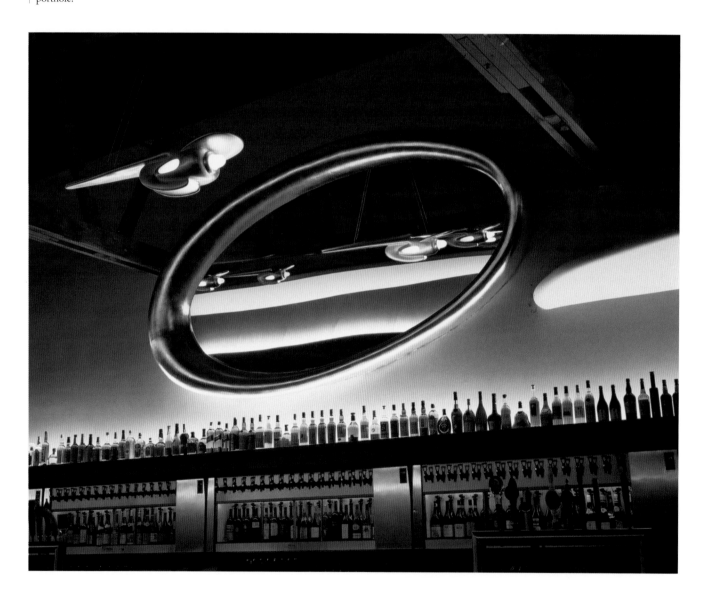

GALLERY

A grain silo acts as a signal for the brewhouse. Bright jewel colors create an anticipation of a good time within.

Photos, this page:
Tim Buchman

The South End Brewery & Smokehouse, by Shook Design Group, is located in a 1930s warehouse in downtown Charlotte, North Carolina. The designers used signage, canopy, and fenestration details to create a vibrant facade and interior that helped revitalize the South End district of the town.

The rather nondescript warehouse as a choice for a restaurant
and bar was a risk on two fronts:
the neighborhood, and the
building structure. Since no
as-builts existed, the architects
had to re-work the exterior with
no knowledge of what lay
beneath the metal-clad exterior.

Photos, this page:
Tim Buchman

The risk paid off. The South End
Brewery & Smokehouse, which
has a lively bar and patio on one
end, and a more formal dining
area at the other, is a vital and
popular night spot.

Located in the central square in Zagreb, Croatia, the facade of the Ban Cafe by Nenad Fabijaníc incorporates red marble from the original 1905 building. While respecting the rhythm of the historic square, the elegant steel-and-glass exterior gives the facade a modern twist that signifies the rebirth of the city.

Photos, this page:
Damir Fabijaníc

In Manhattan's busy meatpacking district, Waterloo, a Belgian restaurant is created from a space with a fifty foot long metal security gate that spanned the entire expanse of the building.

Photos, this page:
Joshua McHugh

Architect Ali Tayar of Parallel Design Partnership created a grid of eight floor-to-ceiling wood-framed glass panels. These slide up and down to serve as windows and doors. Acid etched for an opaque look, the panels create an enticing, glowing facade.

Drawing upon the ambience of ancient Buddhist temples, Zen Palate's patina copper door opens to a quiet niche that sets the tone for the restaurant, where suspended structural bridges constructed of I-beams and mahogany wood planks connect one dining area to another.

Photos, this page:
Norman McGrath

Zen Palate is an international vegetarian restaurant located in a three-story freestanding building facing New York City's bustling Union Square. Designer Tony Chi installed a copper doorway and a juxtaposition of unusual colors to create an eye-catching structure with an unusual entry experience.

The facade, in midtown Manhattan, was divided into two separate and entirely disparate retail spaces. In designing Mangia, both spaces were merged to create a three-story restaurant that occupies the entire ground level. Designers Fellows/ Martinez Architects created a custom steel-and-glass facade.

Photos, this page:
Anton Martinez, AIA

The steel and glass custom ladder has a two-to-one ratio, which creates a symmetry and maintains a reasonable scale at the pedestrian level.

Colette's immaculately detailed transparent entrance is designed as a frame to the street. Stainless-steel details, such as the beam for the letters and the lights embedded in the floor, give the small store a sophisticated air.

Situated on Naples's Via Duomo, an eighteenth-century street located on the ruins of ancient Neapolis, the exclusive womenswear store Colette, designed by Sandro Raffone, has a modern design, but its classical proportions are a witty reference to the street's—and the city's—past.

Photos, this page:
Sandro Raffone

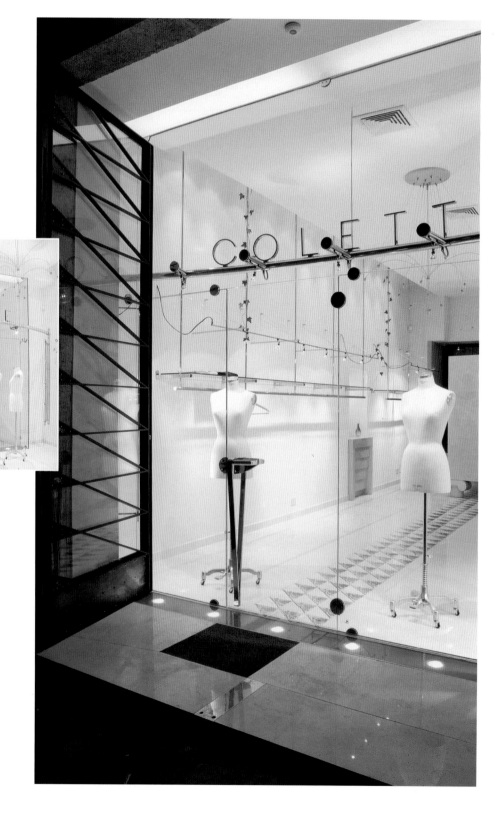

During the course of creating the foundation for the store on this historical street, the workers uncovered huge cisterns dating from Greek times. Although the architect was unable to use fragments of this in the store, he has employed earth colors and the proportions of the Golden Mean to allude to this amazing discovery.

Photos, this page:
Sandro Raffone

The popular San Francisco restaurant Globe is located in a freestanding building that originally housed a blacksmith's shop. The restaurant's facade and name derives from the three dimensional sign, designed and fabricated by Zack Architecture, and inspired by the owner's fascination with the New York City World Fair.

Photos, this page:
J.D. Peterson

The facade of the Universal Cafe in San Francisco, designed and fabricated by Jeff and Larissa Sand of South Park Fabricators consists of windows that pivot both inside and out on specially fabricated pivot hinges, and a glass and wire mesh canopy that reinterprets the Parisian awning.

Monsoon, a restaurant in Santa
Monica, California, serves the
cuisine of Southeast Asia. A large
entry mural serves as a gateway
into this informal and exotic cafe
designed by O'Brien and
Associates.

Photo:
David Glomb

At Paci, a historically listed railroad station converted into a restaurant in Southport, Connecticut, exposed brick and ceiling trusses effectively retain the integrity and charm of the building while subtle colors, lights, and signs signal the change in function. Architect Roger Ferris of Ferris Architects added a steel front-entry stoop, apparently detached from the existing structure.

Photos, this page:
Michael Moran

In the interior, a maple structure—a building within a building—houses the bar and service areas. The dimensions of the interior structure match those of a typical railroad boxcar.

The kitchen is contained behind
a wall, which serves as a screen
for a projected clock image,
a homage to the ubiquitous
station clock.

For the architect, the challenge
was to design an entrance that
would provide a hint of the elegant dining experience inside,
without interfering with the
integrity–or the picturesque
charm–of the station building.

Photos, this page:
Michael Moran

Photo:
Aerial Innovations/
Penny Rogo photos

Lighting articulates architecture. Lighting can be used to dramatize, to highlight, to reveal, to announce. But it can be used just as successfully to do the opposite. Lighting can be used to conceal, to cover, to create shadows and mystery.

In retail stores and in restaurants, designers rely on lighting to create the mood. Dimly lit restaurants with warm, incandescent lamps have played an active role in many a

ANIMATED BY LIGHT

marriage proposal. Bustling cafes and bistros usually exhibit the flash and drama of brighter lights. In retail, where perception of the product is critical to sales, the intensity and color rendition of the light source and a delicate balance of task and ambient lighting takes on a larger significance. Window displays are central to the design of shop entrances, and lighting the display merchandise is critical to consumer walk-ins.

Neon, outdoor floods, quartz spotlights and color filters, and, more recently, laser beams are the most commonly used means of illuminating facades and entrances.

Photo:
Kim Yong Kwan

In the past few years theatrical lighting—as seen in Planet Hollywood and FAO Schwarz in this chapter—has begun seeping into interior and architectural design. Theatrical strobes and floods, according to lighting designer Bill Schwinghammer of Johnson Schwinghammer Lighting Consultants, are being increasingly used at entrances to megastores and high-budget restaurants across the country. Although Schwinghammer agrees that these bring glamour and mystery to the objects they light, he cautions that the fixtures are expensive and need a lot of maintenance.

A successful lighting design goes beyond the large neon sign, or the color flood, to create layers and patterns of light and shadow.

FAO SCHWARZ

Project
FAO Schwarz

Location
Las Vegas, NV USA

Architect
J. Newbold & Associates

Lighting Designers
Johnson Schwinghammer
Lighting Consultants

Photographer
Peter Paige Photography

In Las Vegas, FAO Schwarz's signature rocking horse was reborn as a flashing, smoking spectacle fit for this city of pure theater. Straddling the entrance of the three-level store at the Forum Shops at Caesar's Palace, the 48-foot-tall (14.6-meter-tall) behemoth draws crowds with its animated performance. The Trojan horse—an allusion to the classical theme of the mall—nods its head, flashes its mane, and blows smoke during the ten-minute show, while characters including teddy bears and a chorus line of dolls appear and disappear through trapdoors.

Lighting for the entire 56,000-square-foot (5,040-square-meter) store was designed by the New York–based firm Johnson Schwinghammer Lighting Consultants. Project manager Bill Schwinghammer employed computer-controlled theatrical lights for the ten-minute show, which runs every thirty minutes. Ten theatrical lighting fixtures manufactured by the High End Company are mounted on the vaulted ceiling and on each side of the doorway. They are motor driven, tilt and rotate 360 degrees, and change colors in synchrony with the music and action. The horse has strobes in its mane and an incandescent lamp in its eye.

The imaginatively conceived horse, which attracts crowds of curious shoppers around the entrance to the store, is constructed of steel concrete and fiberglass.

Designed by J. Newbold and Associates of New York, the FAO Schwarz store presents an animated wonderland for children of all ages. Shoppers enter the interactive shop of "The Lost World" through a giant dinosaur ribcage, where raptors roar and rattle their cages. The weighing station at the candy store is comprised of over-scaled candy pieces and "candy mutants," and a beeping spaceship leads into the Star Wars shop.

GALLERIA

Project
Galleria

Location
Seoul, Korea

Lighting Designer
Ener Ken

Photographer
Kim Yong Kwan

Amid the crush of steel, glass, and neon of metropolitan Seoul, the Galleria holds its own. In fact, the exclusive shopping center, with its glowing facade, is a glamorous landmark. "It has become a favorite nighttime backdrop of local soap operas," says Craig A. Roeder, whose Korean firm Ener Ken designed the new facade's lighting.

The Galleria is an elegant 1920s classical building that houses high-end shops such as Hermes and Escada. Retained to give the mall a new image, Roeder and his partner, John Robertson, concentrated on using light to articulate the architecture. "It was a gorgeous piece of architecture to light," says Roeder.

The entire building is generously lit with newly available 3000K metal-halide lamps. Concealed in the overhang atop the building and on an intermediate ledge, cold neon lights yield the glow that defines the elevation. The entrance columns are framed with five 3000K, ten-degree spots with dichroic blue filters that match the blue of the Galleria signage. This, according to Roeder, was a painstaking job, as the building is set at a slight incline. Above each window a striking display of clear quartz lamps in custom-designed fixtures creates sunbursts that highlight the glowing building.

In Seoul, Korea, a high-end
shopping arcade, The Galleria,
has been given a new vitality
with the help of a dramatically
lit facade.

Attention to detail–lights in
nooks and crannies and above
and below ledges–creates different areas of interest in the glowing facade of the building.

Backlit windows, created with
the help of fluorescent tubes
located below window walls add
a three dimensional element to
the lighting design.

GALLERY

In Laredo, Texas, the entrance to Bombay Connection, a store by New York designer Tarik Currimbhoy, is dominated by a large cylindrical display window flanked by two doors with curved canopies.

Photo:
Peter Paige Photography

The sensuous curves of Bombay Connection's central cylinder are highlighted by a red neon strip, while glass blocks create a beacon of light.

Photos, this page:
Peter Paige Photography

Bombay Connection's complex layering of colors and textures results from reflections of cold neon, the reds and blues of the exterior, and the warm glow of the interior reflecting on glass-and-steel surfaces.

The first freestanding structure
of the flamboyant Planet
Hollywood chain by celebrity
designer David Rockwell,
Orlando's earthlike dome is
illuminated by 48 AR500s—
programmable, color-changing
outdoor floodlights—strategi-
cally located in the surrounding
lagoon.

Photo:

Aerial Innovations/
Penny Rogo photos

Lighting designer Craig A.
Roeder gave the Coronado, an
aging retail mall in Albuquerque,
New Mexico, new life with the
use of colorful illumination.
A rainbow of lights against the
adjoining wall generates the
excitement of arrival.

Photo:
Robert Ames Cook photos

An elegant steel and glass canopy designed by Adams-Mohler defines the entrance to the Starbucks building in Seattle. A strip fluorescent sign light above the canopy casts a diffused glow through the glass.

Photos, this page:
James Fredrick Housel

In the Starbucks lobby, a structural column was turned into a light sculpture by designer Brent Markee. Composed of hand-blown glass leaves and copper tubing branches, the sculpture is illuminated with Line Voltage Designer 75 spots, which cast a pattern of light and shadow on the concrete floor.

An oversized pink neon sign at the entrance to the Betsey Johnson's Manhattan showroom gives the customer a taste of the fashion designer's flamboyant style. The interior, designed by Tarik Currimbhoy and Betsey Johnson is a heady mix of colors, textures and patterns.

Photo:
Peter Paige

In Charlotte, North Carolina,
the Lighting Wall designed by
the Connecticut-based firm of
Haverson Architecture and
Design signals a lively restaurant
named the Si! Piazza within the
eight-story office building.

Photos, this page:
Paul Warchol

Custom stained-glass panels that
wrap around the building facade
are back-lit with warm fluorescent strips at top and bottom
and placed in a trough with
reflectors. An even wash of light
thus filters through the colorful,
translucent panels.

The lighted landscape of fountains, spirals, and columns is choreographed by designer John Levy to a seven-minute sound-and-light show that attracts large crowds of onlookers to Bally's.

At the Bally's Resort and Casino, illuminated pylons stretch across the landscape like a space-age interpretation of the columns that once lead to ancient temples and mansions.

Photos, this page:
Dana Anderson,
Allen Photographics

Photo:
Robert Ames Cook

In the vast American suburban sprawl, the shopping mall reigns supreme as a place of community and congregation. In the post–World War II consumer-oriented cultural landscape, the shopping mall substitutes for the village square.

It is appropriate then, that the entrances to malls be heralded by the fanfare of bright lights, flags, and big pavilions, as in the projects shown in this chapter.

FROM THE INSIDE LOOKING IN

Because malls are so representative of the American culture envied around the world, those in other countries, including Mexico and Japan, are built on the American template.

The megamalls built over the past two decades are equipped with atriums and plazas, places expressly designed for people to hang about, to see and be seen in, between purchases of shirts and vacuum cleaners.

Steps into the twenty-first century, perhaps, are the two food court lobbies, Chelsea Market, and the Factory Building, presented here. With the assumption that malls are built to elevate, excite, and offer more than shopping, the two lobbies incorporate contemporary, site-specific sculpture as an integral part of the design.

Photo:
Charles Bechtold

Both projects were developed by Irwin B. Cohen and built by architect Jeff Vandeberg. The two projects are unique in that they do not take themselves seriously. Both feature rather unconventional site-specific sculpture that slyly comments on the decay and debris that go hand in hand with urban consumerist culture. "It would not be possible to do this without the vision of the developer," says Vandeberg, who sets up the rules of the design, and then, "as in a good jazz score," allows the masons, welders, and artists involved freedom to improvise.

SCOTTSDALE MALL

Project
Scottsdale Mall

Location
South Bend, Indiana

Architect
SDI.HTL Inc.

Lighting Designer
Craig A. Roeder Associates

Photographer
Robert Ames Cook

With its flying birds, banners, elevator fountain, and colorful pools, the Scottsdale Mall is meant to be a village square for the 1990s—a festival of fantasy for the entire family between shopping for shirts and toys.

The mall was designed around the theme of bringing the outdoors indoors. The renovation by the Cincinnati-based architecture firm SDI.HTL includes both architectural elements (clerestories, a vaulted roof) and decorative additions such as graphic birds suspended by invisible nylon cables and a fountain elevator in a pool. These, in conjunction with the creative layering and changing colors of Craig Roeder's lighting design, enliven the entire two-story mall.

A pivotal design element is a brightly lit elevator shaft from which water cascades into a pool. Clusters of quartz spots with dichroic color filters, set in the pool, work on a four-circuit cross-fader that moves from magenta to turquoise to white. Topped by a halo of neon rings, the elevator shaft, which connects floor to ceiling—or to be more fanciful, earth to sky—plays as a freestanding sculpture.

Bright colors, large graphic signs and potted plants lend a festive air to the mall plaza. The birds, suspended from the ceiling with invisible cables, are given definition and shadow with the help of luminaires hidden behind trusses.

In the daytime, newly added sky-
lights bring natural light into the
plaza. The elevator shaft, with its
changing array of colors, injects a
dynamic element into the space.

THE FACTORY BUILDING

Project
The Factory Building

Location
Long Island City, NY

Architect
Jeff Vandeberg

Photographer
Charles Bechtold

An eccentric cityscape addition is the Leaning Tower of Long Island City, which stands outside the Factory Building, a former warehouse that now houses a food court, stores, and light manufacturing firms.

"The developer wanted to put something large and distinctive to mark the entrance," says architect Jeff Vandeberg. "He was about to buy an airplane wing, when we hit upon this simple solution." The humorous—and award-winning—project was to rescue an abandoned water tower, paint it bright yellow and red, and rest it on a tilted base. "The water tower is common to the New York skyscape. To bring it down to earth, and tilt it, is to imply that something unusual is going on inside," says Vandeberg.

And it is. To enliven the building's 18,000-square-foot (1,620-square-meter) lobby and to entertain visitors, three artists created a sculpture out of recycled materials, scrap, and abandoned appliances. The extremely fanciful installation includes a huge silver fish, a yellow monster hand, a moon that opens to reveal an astronaut with a trash can head, a bathtub sun, and many less identifiable—but no less enjoyable—objects.

The Leaning Tower won the 1977 Design Excellence Award from the Soceity of American Registered Architects. The President, Michael J. Macaluso said it "brought a smile" to his face everyday on his way to work.

The elevators of the warehouse building were located at the end of a long, featureless corridor.

Three sculptors, John Swing, John Carter, and John Veronis given a free hand to construct site-specific sculpture within the space, have spent years creating and maintaining the fanciful design.

The sculpture in the building has been the subject of a historic lawsuit. In the late eighties, a new developer acquired the building, and wanted to remove the sculpture on the grounds that it was a health hazard. The sculptors won the case, and the installation remains to edify and entertain visitors.

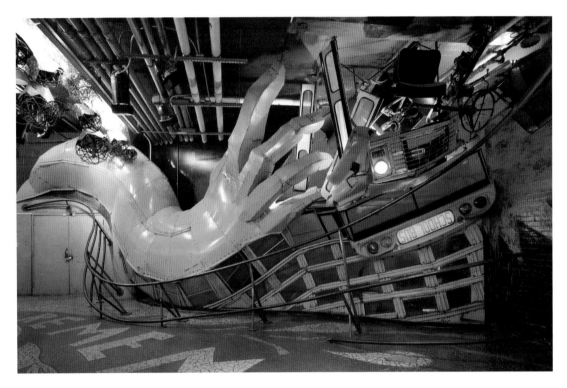

The lobby directory, encrusted in scrap metal and old tools, serves to lead visitors through the fantasy-inspired experience. The normal exchange of information found in almost every company lobby has been elevated here, from the banal to the surreal.

GALLERY

The Pavilions at Buckland Hills
is a 900,000-square-foot
(81,000-square-meter) megamall
with 142 shops and restaurants
located north of Hartford,
Connecticut. At the entrance,
Cambridge Seven Associates created a striking visual image by
constructing pavilions of white,
translucent fabric.

Photo:
Warren Jagger

Having the dubious distinction of being the largest regional shopping center in the country, Franklin Mills in Philadelphia is a two-million-square-foot (180,000-square-meter) mall. The bright, playful entrance by Cambridge Seven Associates makes references to Philadelphia landmarks and history.

Photo:

Warren Jagger

Part of a major waterfront development in Osaka, Japan, the Tempozan Marketplace, designed by Cambridge Seven Associates, is a three-level building in which the facade reinforces the maritime character of the area with the use of colorful banners resembling nautical pendants.

Photo:

H. Culpen

In Pasona, a venetian glass store in a Tokyo shopping mall designed by Yoshimi Kono of Vignelli Associates, the colorful wares are treated as art objects.

Photos, this page:
Nacasa and Partners

In this ingeniously designed space, three walls of individually lit glass objects form a triangle that succeeds in eliminating the traditional entry sequence, turning the entire shop into a pristine display area.

The unique qualities of light and water in the Gulf Coast inspired the decor of University Mall in Tampa, Florida. At the entrance to the food courts, lighting designed by Craig A. Roeder and Associates mimics light reflecting on water.

Photo:
Robert Ames Cook

In Mexico City, a modern furniture store in the Santa Fe, an American-style shopping mall, boasts an entrance whose meticulous detailing signals the quality of the designed objects sold within.

Photos, this page:
Luis Goroda

Designed by Aevum Arquitectura y Diseno, the entrance to Points is dominated by a massive lacewood curved door with metal accents that ultimately represents the store's identity.

The Chelsea Market block in Manhattan is a collection of eighteen separate buildings totaling one million square feet (90,000 square meters) that were originally the offices of the National Biscuit Company. A catenary arch forms the connection between the buildings.

Photo:

James Shanks

In the creative renovation by Jeff Vandeberg, the rough, unfinished quality of natural materials is complemented by sculptures and artwork throughout the lobby of the space, in which vendors purvey mainly specialty foods.

Photo:
James Shanks

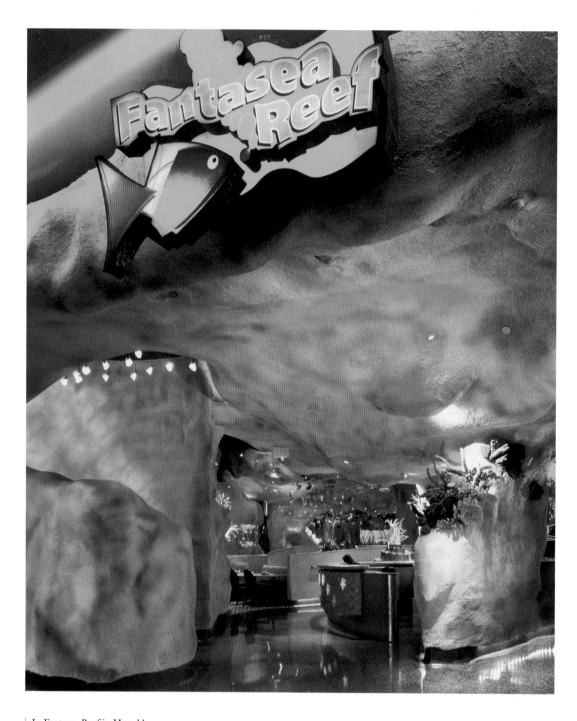

In Fantasea Reef in Harrah's
Atlantic City, Daroff Design created a whimsical interpretation
of an underwater coral reef. Blue
cold-cathode lighting and pattern projectors illuminate the
ceiling to convey the depth and
movement of the ocean.

Photo:
Elliot Kaufman

At Famous Players' SilverCity in
Toronto, a state-of-the-art movie
palace, food kiosks are treated to
almost every conceivable pattern
and color. The design by International Design Group is chaotic,
yet there's method in the mad-
ness: each feature is a unique
design and the discord creates
an animated fantasyland.

Photo:
Robert Burley
Design Archive

A circular, plastic partition greets customers as they walk into the store. The translucent back-lit partition serves as an intriguing entrance that provides a tiny, tantalizing hint of the space within.

Photos, this page:
Farshid Assassi

Located in a typical faceless suburban shopping strip in Des Moines, Iowa, the M.C. Ginsberg Objects of Art is a flexible, gallery like space.

The existing space was gutted to the perimeter walls and steel joist roof structure. All materials and cabinets are anchored by stainless steel bolts and security screws so that materials can be reconstructed in another space when the current lease expires.

The architects, Herbert Lewis Kruse Blunk have used plain, unfinished materials such as unpainted cement board, rough concrete, unfinished plywood to create a rough space that would contrast with the gold, silver and precious stones on display.

Photos, this page:
Farshid Assassi

Photo:
Daniel Aubry

A burger in Bombay, pasta primavera in Kuala Lumpur, surf and turf (with ketchup, please) in Japan—this is the global village, where cultures collide and merge and are formed anew. Now, on the edge of the millennium, the global village is based on information—and in design, information translates into signals. How do we signal American fast food in Bombay, Chinese food in Melbourne? How does we indicate a specialty through the design of an entrance?

SPECIALLY DESIGNED

Strip down a culture or concept and simplify it into a recognizable signal. Stars and steel mean America, water flowing into large pots evokes ancient Asian villages. In Surf and Turf, designer Jordan Mozer employs subtle, humorous signs to create an American setting. The front door, which is copper and rounded like a cartoon form, has a cast-bronze door pull in the shape of a cartoon character's extended hand; in Japan, a country where people bow, one must shake hands to enter this Western restaurant.

Felissimo is a Japanese store in midtown Manhattan selling a rather esoteric collection of designed objects, all loosely grouped together to appeal to the ecologically conscious customer. How does one get this complex message across amid the crush of stimuli on a New York street? Designer Clodagh uses leaves to signal nature and ecology and elaborate, handcrafted fixtures and finishes to denote luxury. "We wanted to create a supportive, calm, enriching atmosphere, with a sense of opulence that you find in nature as you do in orchids or a peach tree," says Clodagh.

On the edge of the millennium, the global culture is not so simple anymore.

Photo:
Tim Griffith

FELISSIMO

Project
Felissimo

Location
New York, NY USA

Designer
Clodagh Design

Photographer
Daniel Aubry

In midtown Manhattan, a set of frosted-glass doors intricately etched with windblown fronds invites attention to Felissimo, a store that sells ecologically conscious crafted products. Located in a six-story 1901 neoclassical townhouse, the store, owned by Japanese entrepreneur Kazuhiko Yasaki, sells an eccentric collection of upscale, designer household artifacts, accessories, linens, and jewelry, all related by virtue of environmental consideration.

The design of Felissimo, by New York designer Clodagh, establishes the ecological theme with the fronds at the entrance and carries it through into the interior with elements such as a giant leaf rug on the third floor, a profusion of plants and fountains, and painted-leaf motifs on the walls.

Handcrafted objects, a trademark of the Irish-born Clodagh, are used throughout the store. From the bronze torchières that flank the entrance to the display units, chandeliers, and wall finishes throughout the store, the objects *of* display are as worthy of attention—if not more so—than the objects *on* display.

Designed by New York city's Grand Central Terminal architects Warren & Wetmore in 1901, the townhouse, now surrounded by towering steel and glass buildings was restored and stained ochre.

Mirrors near the entryway are a
result of a suggestion made by
an expert in *feng shui*, the Asian
art of room design and furniture
placement. The handcrafted door
is flanked by handcrafted torchiers.

Collaborating with over fifty
artists, and craftspeople, Clodagh
has used around eighty-five custom-made fixtures, finishes and
fittings–all made up of environ-
mentally friendly materials and
finishes–in the 12,000 square
foot (1114.8 square-meter) space.

JOYCE

Project
Joyce

Location
Hong Kong, China

Designer
Tsao & McKown

Photographers
Tim Griffith & Jen Fong

The Joyce store in Hong Kong is a part of a chain that sells exclusive designer clothing and accessories throughout Southeast Asia. Behind the retail empire is Joyce Ma, who, twenty-five years ago, hit on the novel idea of bringing Versace and Armani to her native Hong Kong. Ma placed the clothing in an intimate, salonlike setting, another unconventional idea for that place and time. Now a fashion doyenne with a successful business, a fashion magazine that carries her name, and an annual turnover of $140 million, Ma retains the New York architectural firm of Tsao & McKown to design all Joyce stores.

In translating Ma's vision into physical space, the designers created a visual vocabulary for her, elements of which are varied to suit different cultures. The Taiwan and Bangkok stores, for example, offer a subtle entrance experience. However, Hong Kong, like New York, is a commercial hub and a melting pot, a place that supports a highly aggressive selling environment. The store thus has a aggressive streetfront identity, with a sense of procession and public promenade. The store is a big, open space, designed like a stage set in which the clothes are the performers.

In the Joyce store in Hong Kong, a long storefront gave the designers an opportunity to create a promenade, a procession which makes the actual act of entry a theatrical experience.

In the interior, vibrant colors, and luxurious finishes set a stage for the exclusive clothes and accessories. Unlike most clothing stores where furniture is usually functional or made to order, Joyce is furnished with expensive, designer pieces individually selected by the designers.

GALLERY

Surf and Turf is an American-
Japanese fusion restaurant located
in Matsuyama, Japan. The design,
by Jordan Mozer and Associates,
makes witty references to American popular culture.

Photos:
Jordan Mozer & Associates

The front door, made of copper
and rounded like a cartoon form,
has a cast-bronze door pull in
the shape of a cartoon character's
extended hand; in a country
where people bow, the hand-
shake signals a foreign cultural
experience within.

The bulging forms of the free-standing concrete gateway with copper finish pop out of the glass tile facade, advertising the restaurant to drivers as they speed by this densely trafficked area.

Americas in Houston, Texas, is a
restaurant that weaves together
the food and cooking of Europe
and South America. The facade,
designed by Jordan Mozer and
Associates, is a wall of woven
exterior gypsum and a sculptural
representation of this concept.
The woven window wall allows
glimpses into the interior.

Photo:
David Clifton

In Scalini's La Piccola Italia, an
Italian restaurant in Kuala
Lumpur, Malaysia, by Tony Chi
& Associates, the doorway and
the front wall are covered with
a sheet of copper. The patina
copper, an uneven green, reflects
on adjacent walls to create a
subtle glow.

Photo:
Paul Warchol

Creative use of copper, stone and
neon creates this "open lodge"
themed western bar and restaurant at in North Kansas City,
Missouri. Located at "The
Range" part of a Harrah's Entertainment chain, the restaurant
was designed by the Hnedak
Bobo Group.

Photo:

Jeff Schotland

In Mumbai, India, the design firm Batliboi Currimbhoy interprets the American fast-food concept with neon, bright colors, and reflective surfaces. The bright America Cafe sign and cafe tables signal the restaurant's menu as people drive by on the busy seafront thoroughfare.

Photos:
Bipin Mistry

The America theme is carried through to the interior with the red, white, and blue colors of the flag and the custom-made steel stars on signs and counters.

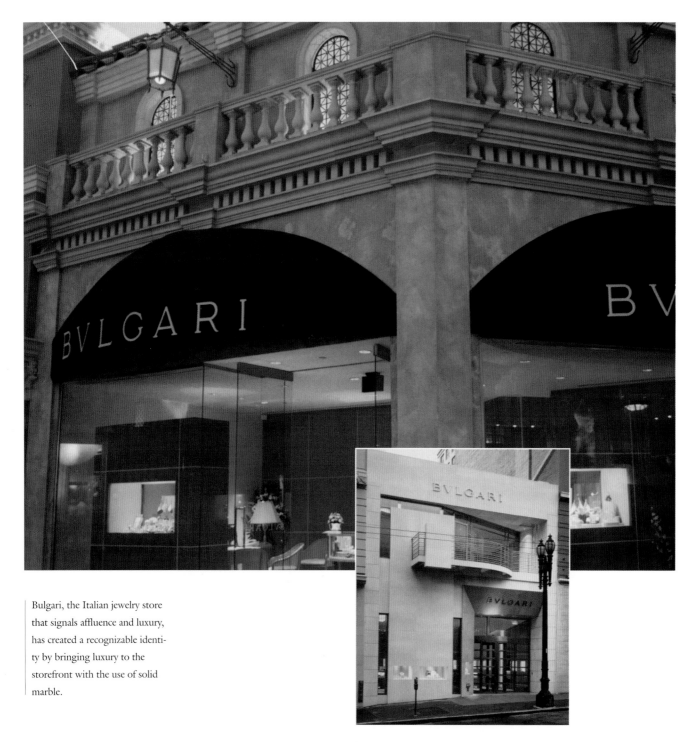

Bulgari, the Italian jewelry store that signals affluence and luxury, has created a recognizable identity by bringing luxury to the storefront with the use of solid marble.

Small, storefront niches featuring exquisite jewelry displays, another trademark of the chain, are a successful strategy to arrest attention of passing pedestrians. The stores featured were all designed by the Milan-based architects Marco Carrano.

Photos, this page:
©Marco Carran

The insertion of the marble cube and portals into buildings as disparate as a Westin Hotel block in Chicago to a landmark building on prestigious Rodeo Drive in Los Angeles is designed to instill a sense of permanence and reliability.

Photos, this page:
©Marco Carran

Constructed of fiberglass and
steel, the giant toys, which were
transported in sections and
assembled on site, create a striking visual image that attracts the
attention of passing cars.

The FAO Schwarz building in
Orlando is part of a new, outdoor shopping center. The challenge for the designer was to create a memorable image with the
assigned 100 foot long 17 foot
high box of a building. Designer
Joanne Newbold's ingenious
solution was to create a toy box
out of the building. The entrance
is flanked by giant paste-up toys.
A 32 foot tall teddy bear, 40 foot
tall raggedy Anne, and other
popular toys

Photos, this page:
Peter Paige

The colorful design has the
advantage of being instantly
recognizable to children, the
group that it aims to attract.

Photos, this page:
Peter Paige Photography

The design of Silk, a Chinese restaurant in Melbourne, Australia, by Tony Chi & Associates, is a pared-back orientalism. At the entrance, a fountain cascading into large pots recalls the traditional entrance experience of Asian villages.

Photos, this page:
George Apostolidis

Located in the Crown Towers, one of Melbourne's high profile, new, luxury hotels, Silk is designed to evoke the sensuality of the East.

A spectacular Mongolian tent of
damask and hand-cut silks serves
as a bar, and becomes the central
focus of the restaurant.

Photos, this page:
George Apostolidis

Adams-Mohler
341412 Freemont Avenue North
Seattle, WA 98103

DIRECTORY OF ARCHITECTS
AND DESIGNERS

Aevum Arquitectura y Diseno
Calle 2 No. 2 Col. Reforma Social
Mexico D.F. 11650
Mexico

Geoffrey Warner
Alchemy Design
2219 Sharon Avenue SE
Minneapolis, MN 55414

Alsop & Störmer Architects (with
Mason Design)
Bishop's Wharf
39-49 Parkgate Road
London SW11 4NP
England

Tarik Currimbhoy
Batliboi Currimbhoy Design
Panday House, Mumbai
India

Bergmeyer Associates
286 Congress Street
Boston, MA 02210

Antonello Boschi, Architetto
Via Colombo 22
58022 Follonica
Italy

C & J Partners, Inc.
One Colorado
36 Hugus Alley
Suite 210
Pasadena, CA 91103

Cambridge Seven Associates, Inc.
1050 Massachusetts Avenue
Cambridge, MA 02138

Tony Chi & Associates
20 West 36th Street
9th Floor
New York, NY 10018

Clodagh Design International
670 Broadway
New York, NY 10012

Currimbhoy Design
833 Broadway #3
New York, NY 10003

Jeffrey Daniels
Jeffrey Daniels & Associates (Formerly Grinstein/Daniels
Architects)
8617 Lookout Mountain Avenue
Los Angeles, CA 90046

Daroff Design Inc.
2300 Ionic Street
Philadelphia, PA 19103

François de Menil
21 East 40th Street #2000
New York, NY 10016

Martin Dorf
Dorf Associates
36 West 25th Street
11th Floor
New York, NY 10010

Ener Ken
c/o Craig A. Roeder Associates
3829 North Hall Street
Dallas, TX 75219

Nenad Fabijaníc
Arhitektonski Studio Fabijaníc
Cujetna Ceesta 9
10 000 Zagreb
Croatia

Fellows/Martinez Architects
988 Second Avenue
New York, NY 10022

Roger Ferris
Ferris Architects PC
90 Post Road East
Westport, CT 06880

Louis Ulrich
FFKR Architecture/Planning/Interior Design
133 Pierpont Avenue
Suite 200
Salt Lake City, UT 84101

Gleicher Design Group/ Larry S. Davis and Associates
7 West 22nd Street, 10th Floor
New York, NY 10010

Haverson Architecture and Design PC
289 Greenwich Avenue
Greenwich, CT 06830

Herbert Lewis Kruse Blunck
202 Fleming Building
Des Moines, IA 50309

Hirsch Bedner Associates
3216 Nebraska Avenue
Santa Monica, CA 90404

Hnedak Bobo Group, Inc.
104 South Front Street
Memphis, TN 38103

International Design Group, Inc.
188 Avenue Road
Toronto, Ontario M5R 2J1
Canada

Joanne Newbold
J. Newbold & Associates
206 East 63rd Street #3
New York, NY 10021

Jordan Mozer & Associates, Ltd.
320 West Ohio Street
7th Floor
Chicago, IL 60610

Last Stop Design Company
1344 Fourth Street
Santa Monica, CA 90401

John Levy
John Levy Lighting Productions
930 Colorado Boulevard
Los Angeles, CA 90041

Lieber Cooper Associates
444 North Michigan Avenue, Suite 1200
Chicago, IL 60611

Marco Carrano Associates
347 Fifth Avenue
New York, NY 10016

Nike Design Team
One Bowerman Drive
Beeverton, OR 97005

Margaret O'Brien
O'Brien + Associates Design Inc.
222 Washington Avenue #12
Santa Monica, CA 90403

Ali Tayar
Parallel Design Partnership
430 West 14th Street
Suite 408
New York, NY 10014

Sandro Raffone
Piazza Gesu E Maria 4
80135 Napoli
Italy

David Rockwell
Rockwell Group
5 Union Square West
New York, NY 10003

Craig A. Roeder Associates
3829 North Hall Street
Dallas, TX 75219

Rogers Marvel Architects
145 Hudson Street
Third Floor
New York, NY 10013

SDI.HTL Inc.
Cincinnati, OH
no address available

Ray M. Simon
1912R Cherokee Street
St. Louis, MO 63118

Shook Design Group
The Atherton Mill
2000 South Boulevard
Suite 510
Charlotte, NC 28203

Jeff and Larissa Sand
South Park Fabricators
136 South Park
San Francisco, CA 94107

SPF:a
4223 Glencoe Avenue
Suite B115
Venice, CA 90292
Los Angeles, CA

Tsao & McKown Architects, PC
20 Vandam Street
10th Floor
New York, NY 10003

II BY IV Design Associates Inc.
77 Mowat Avenue
Suite 109
Toronto, Ontario M6K 3E3
Canada

Jeff Vandeberg
873 Broadway
New York, NY 10003

Yoshimi Kono
Vignelli Associates
475 Tenth Avenue
New York, NY 10018

Walt Disney Imagineering/Jordon Mozer and Associates
1401 Flower Street
Glendale, CA 91221

Zack Architecture
161 Natoma Street
San Francisco, CA 94105

Aerial Innovations/ Penny Rogo
1413 South Howard Avenue
Suite 206
Tampa, FL 33606

DIRECTORY OF PHOTOGRAPHERS

Dana Anderson/Allen Photographics
c/o John Levy Lighting Productions
930 Colorado Boulevard
Los Angeles, CA 90041

George Apostolidis
c/o Tony Chi & Associates
20 West 36th Street
9th Floor
New York, NY 10018

Farshid Assassi
Assassi Productions
P. O. Box 3651
Santa Barbara, CA 93105

Daniel Aubry
c/o Clodagh Design International
670 Broadway
New York, NY 10012

Mark Ballogg of Steincamp/Ballogg
666 W. Hubbard
Chicago, IL 60610

Charles Bechtold
1162 St. Georges Avenue
Suite 286
Avenel, NJ 07001

Tom Bonner Photography
1201 Abbot Kinney Boulevard
Venice, CA 90291

Tim Buchman
1311-L Corton Drive
Charlotte, NC 28203

Alessandro Ciampi
c/o Antonello Boschi, Architetto
Via Colombo 22
58022 Follonica
Italy

David Clifton
26/37 West Winnemac
Chicago, IL 60625

Robert Ames Cook
c/o Craig A. Roeder Associates
3829 North Hall Street
Dallas, TX 75219

Roderick Coyne
c/o Alsop & Störmer Architects
Bishop's Wharf
39-49 Parkgate Road
London SW11 4NP
England

H. Culpen
c/o Cambridge Seven Associates, Inc.
1050 Massachusetts Avenue
Cambridge, MA 02138

Robert Burley/Design Archive
c/o International Design Group, Inc.
188 Avenue Road
Toronto, Ontario M5R 2J1
Canada

Damir Fabijaníc
c/o Arhitektonski Studio Fabijaníc
Cujetna Ceesta 9
10 000 Zagreb
Croatia

David Glomb
71340 Estellita
Rancho Mirage, CA 92270

Luis Goroda
c/o Aevum Arquitectura y Diseno
Calle 2 No. 2 Col. Reforma Social
Mexico D.F. 11650
Mexico

Tim Griffith
c/o Tsao & McKown Architects, PC
20 Vandam Street
10th Floor
New York, NY 10003

Steven Hall/Hedrich Blessing
11 West Illinois
Chicago, IL 60610

Hirsch Bedner Associates
3216 Nebraska Avenue
Santa Monica, CA 90404

James Fredrick Housel
Housel Photography
2307 Shoreland Drive South
Seattle, WA 98144

Jordan Mozer
c/o Jordan Mozer & Associates, Ltd.
320 West Ohio Street
7th Floor
Chicago, IL 60610

Itochu Fashion System
c/o Rogers Marvel Architects
145 Hudson Street
3rd Floor
New York, NY 10013

Warren Jagger Photography, Inc.
150 Chestnut Street
7th Floor
Providence, RI 02903

Richard Johnson/Interior Images
c/o The International Design Group, Inc.
188 Avenue Road
Toronto, Ontario M5R 2J1
Canada

Douglas Kahn
P. O. Box 1430
Westcliffe, CO 81252

Elliott Kaufman
873 Broadway
New York, NY 10003

Scott Kohno
c/o C & J Partners, Inc.
One Colorado
36 Hugus Alley
Suite 210
Pasadena, CA 91103

Kim Yong Kwan
c/o Craig A. Roeder Associates/Ener Ken
3829 North Hall Street
Dallas, TX 75219

Chun Y. Lai
119 West 23rd Street
Studio 905
New York, NY 10011

Mark Lohman Photography
1021 South Fairfax
Los Angeles, CA 90019

Anton Martinez
Fellows/Martinez Architects
988 Second Avenue
New York, NY 10022

Lynne Massimo
c/o Rogers Marvel Architects
145 Hudson Street
3rd Floor
New York, NY 10013

Norman McGrath
164 West 79th Street
New York, NY 10024

Joshua McHugh
111 Fourth Avnue
Suite 4K
New York, NY 10003

Karen Melvin Photography
605 7th Street S.E.
Minneapolis, MN 53414

Bipin Mistry
c/o Batliboi Currimbhoy Design
Panday House, Mumbai
India

Grant Mudford
2660 Dundee Place
Los Angeles, CA 90027

Nacasa and Partners
305-5 Minami Azabu
Minato, Tokyo
Japan

Peter Paige Photography
269 Parkside road
Harrington Park, NJ 07640

J.D. Peterson
530 Hampshire #303
San Francisco, CA 94110

Sandro Raffone
Piazza Gesu E Maria 4
80135 Napoli
Italy

Jeff Schotland
Hnedak Bobo Group, Inc.
104 South Front Street
Memphis, TN 38103

James Shanks
153 Norfolk #4E
New York, NY 10002

Dominique Vorillon
c/o Rogers Marvel Architects
145 Hudson Street
3rd Floor
New York, NY 10013

Paul Warchol Photography
133 Mulberry Street #6S
New York, NY 10013

David Whittaker Photography
444 Heath Street East
Toronto, Ontario M4G 1B5
Canada

Nayana Currimbhoy is a New York-based free-
lance writer who has been writing about architecture and design since 1984.

ABOUT THE AUTHOR

She was Special Features Editor at *Interiors*
magazine, and is a regular contributor at
Architectural Record.

Currimbhoy is also the author of two books,
Indira Gandhi, a Biography and *Living in
Deserts,* both published by Grolier.

She is currently working on a book about
women in ancient India.